SOME PEOPLE...

by Mary Callery Carlson
illustrated by Jack Proctor

Tyndale House
Publishers, Inc.
Wheaton, Illinois

Coverdale House
Publishers, Ltd.
Eastbourne, England

To Tom and Janey

All Scripture quotations are taken from *The Living Bible,* © 1971 by Tyndale House Publishers, Wheaton, Illinois. **Some People.** Library of Congress Catalog Card Number 76-8669. ISBN 0-8423-6060-3, cloth. Copyright © 1976 Mary J. Carlson. All rights reserved. Second printing, December 1976. Printed in the United States of America.

Contents

OBEDIENT CARE

JOYFUL TRUTHFUL

THOUGHTFUL

UNDERSTANDING GENTLE

KIND FRIENDLY

HONEST LOYAL

HOSPITABLE PATIENT

FORGIVING GENEROUS

RESPONSIBLE THANKFUL

LOVING

Dear Mom and Dad:

This is a "children's book"—for *parents!* We want to help you develop biblical character traits in your child. Each page emphasizes specific biblical principles that God intended man to apply in the development of Christian character.

Generation after generation of people struggle to develop and implement a program or system that will establish "good will toward men"—a system that God gave in the Bible from the very beginning! Still the struggle continues—except for *Some People...*

This book is much more than words and pictures. Here is a suggestion for its most effective use: The illustrations are intended to serve as visual aids for the child and to stimulate interest. After you, the reader, have completed the reading of a character trait, discuss the coordinating picture-scene. Ask the child, or children, to repeat the trait-word and to think of different situations that would apply to *that* word.

This is a book that can *live* and *give* forever in the life of your child. It presents the teachings of Jesus in a unique manner, making it one of the most important and meaningful books you can read with your child. *Some People* should be shared with ... *all people.*

In his love,

Mary Carlson

May God's mercy and peace be upon all of you who live by this principle and upon those everywhere who are really God's own.
Galatians 6:16, *The Living Bible*

Some people are....

Some people...

know God

      and...

                they love him!

The Bible tells us...

      he

      is

      our

      Father

      in

      heaven...

                and...

he loves us very much.

Some people

know

"God made the world...
the heaven and sea.
He made everything...
for *you* and *me*."

       Some people know it...
       their lives show it.

"God guides our lives
so carefully.
We're his children,
you and *me*."

       Some people know it...
       their lives show it.

"God loves ... he knows,
and *he* can see...
the way we live,
you and *me*."

       Some people know it
          and
       here's how they show it...

Some people

CARE

about the world...
The whole wide world...
and everything that's in it!
The people
the land
the sky
the water
the animals
the food
the colors
the rain
the snow ... and ...
many other things.
Some people care about *you.*
What
do
you
care
about?
God is pleased with people, when
they
care.

Some people are

OBEDIENT

They try to obey God in everything.
They obey their
mothers and fathers.
They obey the laws
of their government.
They learn what God wants them to do...
by reading his instructions
in the
Bible.
They follow God's teaching...
in the way they talk,
in the way they act,
in the way they think...
and in the things they do.
God is pleased with them, because...
they
are
obedient.

OBEY me and live! Guard
my words as your most precious
possession.
Proverbs 7:2

Some people are

TRUTHFUL

They
are honest in what they say.
They
do
not
lie.
They
keep
their
promises.
They do not gossip about other people.
When they speak, they are fair
and say only what they know to be true.
People trust them and believe what they say.
God is pleased with them, because...
they
are
truthful.

Stop lying to each other;
tell the TRUTH, for we are
parts of each other and when
we lie to each other we are
hurting ourselves.
Ephesians 4:25.

Some people are

JOYFUL

They are happy and cheerful,
because they know God loves and cares for them.

They

are

not

crabby.

People

are

happy

to

be

with

them.

They enjoy life,
because they try to please God and...
God has promised *his* "joy" to all those who obey him.

God is pleased with them, because...

they

are

joyful.

*For God gives to those
who please him ... wisdom,
knowledge, and JOY.*
Ecclesiastes 2:26

Some people are

THOUGHTFUL OF OTHERS

They try to get along with other people.
They join others in playing games ... and

                      they
                      follow
                      the rules.

They don't sulk in a corner
and make others unhappy,
because they can't have their own way.

      They are
      not stubborn.
      They take turns watching TV programs.
      They put the cap back on
      the toothpaste tube.

They have happy homes, because they play and work together.

      God is pleased with them, because...

           they
           are
           thoughtful of others.

*In response to all God has done
for us, let us outdo each other
in being helpful and kind to each
other and doing good.* Hebrews 10:24

Some people are

UNDERSTANDING

They try to know how others think and feel.
They try to know why people do the things they do.
When someone makes a mistake ... and

breaks

a

dish

or

a

new

toy ... they are

forgiving.

They are understanding with their parents, too ... so,
they don't cry and beg them for things they

know

they

can't

have!

They *really* listen, when other people have an idea.
They try to see another person's side of things.

God is pleased with them, because...

they

are

understanding.

*How wonderful to be wise,
to UNDERSTAND things, to
be able to analyze them and
interpret them. Wisdom lights
up a man's face, softening its
hardness.* Ecclesiastes 8:1

Some people are

GENTLE

They speak softly and listen patiently.
They try to comfort people who are sad.
Their words are kind.
Their actions are peaceable.

> They
> are
> not
> mean.

They are calm...
and carefully help someone who has been hurt.

> They
> are
> not
> rough!

They are gentle with animals, too.
They help make others feel comfortable.

> God is pleased with them, because...

> **they**
> **are**
> **gentle.**

*GENTLE words cause
life and health.*
Proverbs 15:4

Some people are

KIND

They cheer people who are sad.
They visit people who are lonely.
They pray with people who are sick ... and sometimes
they send them
a gift or a card.

If they see that someone is hurt,
they try to help.
If they see someone make a foolish mistake,
they do not laugh and embarrass him or her.
If they see that someone is afraid ... or bashful,
they encourage him.
If they see someone crying,
they ask if they can help ... they do not
walk away and
leave him
alone.

They care about others' feelings.
God is pleased with them, because...
**they
are
kind.**

*When others are happy, be
happy with them. If they
are sad, share their sorrow.*
Romans 12:15

Some people are

FRIENDLY

They like you just the way you are!
They don't stare at people
who look or dress differently than they do.
They help people feel comfortable.
If someone has hurt them ... and
says, "Please forgive me. I'm
sorry," they accept the apology.
They do *not* get upset and pout,
if others don't agree with them.
They *greet* people with a smile
and
people enjoy being with them.
God is pleased with them, because
they
are
friendly.

A true FRIEND is always loyal,
and a brother is born to help
in time of need.
Proverbs 17:17

Some people are

HONEST

Their actions show it.
When playing games, they do not cheat!
    They do
    not steal.
They can be trusted ... they
                    are
                    not
                    snoopy!
If they make a mistake, they admit it ... and do not
                                blame others.

They know God sees everything they do.
They realize God knows their thoughts, too.
    God is pleased with them, because...
        they
        are
        honest.

Never forget to be TRUTHFUL
and kind. Hold these virtues
tightly. Write them deep
within your heart.
Proverbs 3:3

Some people are

LOYAL

They are faithful to their families,
    to their friends, and
    to their country...
They are ready to help, whenever there is a need.
They do not
just pretend to
be a friend.
  Nor do they talk
  unkindly about others
  behind their backs.
People can count on them, because...
  they are trustworthy.
  They are true friends.
  They are reliable.
  God is pleased with them, because...
    they
    are
    loyal.

*If you love someone, you
will be LOYAL to him no matter
what the cost. You will always
believe in him, always expect
the best of him, and always stand
your ground in defending him.*
1 Corinthians 13:7

Some people are

HOSPITABLE

They cheerfully ask people to come to their homes...
and they make them feel welcome.
If someone comes to their home, without
being asked, they gladly invite him to come in
and offer him something to eat.

Their homes are always open
to those who need help.

They give water to those who are thirsty.
They share food with those who are hungry.
They offer a bed to those who have no place to sleep.
They take care of those who are sick.
They share their time with those who are lonely.

God is pleased with them, because...

they
are
hospitable.

Cheerfully share your home
with those who need a meal
or a place to stay for the night.
1 Peter 4:9

Some people are

PATIENT

They are calm and gentle.
When others keep them waiting, they
                                    do
                                    not
                                    grumble.
When waiting in line ... or playing a game, they
                                    do
                                    not
                                    push
                                    and
                                    shove.

          They wait until it's their turn!
They stick with a job, until it gets done well.
          They do not lose their temper and shout
          when something goes wrong.
If others are slow to understand,
they do not get angry.
Instead, they go over the matter again.
They live peacefully with other people.
          God is pleased with them, because...
          they
          are
          patient.

*Dear brothers, warn those who
are lazy; comfort those who are
frightened; take tender care of
those who are weak; and be
PATIENT with everyone.*
1 Thessalonians 5:14

Some people are

FORGIVING

They are willing to forget
an unkind word or deed.
When someone hurts them, they

> do
> not
> *stay*
> angry.

They try to understand *why* someone said
or did the thing that hurt them.

> They
> don't
> hold
> grudges!
> They try to make things *right!*

People who are able to forgive and forget
others' faults or mistakes are happy people.

> God is pleased with them, because...

> **they**
> **are**
> **forgiving.**

Be gentle and ready to FORGIVE;
never hold grudges. Remember,
the Lord forgave you, so you
must forgive others.
Colossians 3:13

Some people are

GENEROUS

They are happy to share what
they have with other people.

> They
> are
> not
> selfish.

They like to give gifts to their friends...
especially "surprise presents!"
They cheerfully give their time
to people who need help.

> They learn to give gladly to others
> without expecting to receive
> something in return.

They are happy when their friends get new toys.

> They
> are
> not
> jealous.

The Bible says, "God loves a cheerful giver."

> God is pleased with them, because...

> > **they**
> > **are**
> > **generous.**

*It is more blessed to
GIVE than to receive.*
Acts 20:35

Some people are

RESPONSIBLE

People can rely on them to do their jobs, everyday ... without always having to be told.

They take care of things they use.
They look after things they own as well as things that belong to others.
>They do not put their feet on the furniture.
>They do not scratch their desks at school.
>They do not write on walls.

They hang up their clothes.
They pick up their toys.
They do their schoolwork.
>They comb their hair and
>brush their teeth ... without fussing
>or making faces.

By doing their part at home and school,
they prove they are *responsible* people.
They can be trusted.
>God is pleased with them, because...
>**they**
>**are**
>**responsible.**

Tackle every task that comes along, and if you fear God you can expect his blessing.
Ecclesiastes 7:18

Sume peuple are

THANKFUL

They are happy to be the person God has made them.
They appreciate their ... family and friends,
home and food,
clothes and toys.
They are glad for puppies and kittens,
and for picnics . . . with hot dogs and
ice cream.
They are grateful for people
who help others ... like ... teachers and doctors,
farmers and policemen.
They are thankful for church, where they learn about Jesus.
They praise God
for their country!
They thank God for all things.
God is pleased with them, because...
they
are
thankful.

*No matter what happens
always be THANKFUL, for
this is God's will for you
who belong to Christ Jesus.*
1 Thessalonians 5:18

Some people are

LOVING

God gives them his special love for other people.
They believe in people...
and expect the best of them.
        People are not
        afraid of them.
They show their love to others in special ways.
Like:

Remembering	Sharing	Obeying
other	their	their
people's	toys.	parents.
birthdays.		

They are not jealous or selfish.
They are not grumpy or mean.
They are generous and patient...
thoughtful and gentle...
hospitable and truthful.
        In these and many other ways they are loving.
God tells us that love is the most important thing of all.
        God is pleased with them, because...

they

are

loving.

Dear friends, let us practice LOVING each other, for LOVE comes from God and those who are LOVING and kind show that they are the children of God, and that they are getting to know him better. 1 John 4:7

And...

      so ... we've learned a little bit about *Some People.*
We know they love God and obey him.

      They treat others with love
                and
                understanding.
They are patient and forgiving.
They are gentle and honest.

      They
      are
      generous
      and
      loyal.

        Oh! ... wouldn't this be a *better* world,
and wouldn't God be *pleased*
        if
we could be like *Some People?*